This Playbook Belongs To Coach:

_____

DEDICATION

This Basketball Playbook Journal Log book is dedicated to all the Basketball Coaches out there who love the game of Basketball & want to record their plays, drills, etc and document their findings in the process.

You are my inspiration for producing books and I'm honored to be a part of keeping all of your Basketball notes and records organized.

This journal notebook will help you record your details about coaching your team.

Thoughtfully put together with these sections to record: 12 Undated Calendar Month Pages, Index of Games, Player Roster, Blank Basketball Court Templates, Statistics at a Glance Pages, and Notes.

How To Use This Book:

The purpose of this book is to keep all of your Basketball notes all in one place. It will help keep you organized.

This Basketball Playbook Journal will allow you to accurately document every detail about coaching your team. It's a great way to chart your course through coaching Champions!

Here are examples of the prompts for you to fill in and write about your experience in this book:

1. Contact Page - Write your name and information.

2. 12 Undated Calendar Month Pages - Undated for your convenience. Month at a glance for organizing practices, games and tournaments.

3. Index of Games - See your game schedule at a glance. Space for Opponent, Date, Location, Win or Loss and Final Score.

4. Player Roster - Record each Team Member also includes space for their Home number and Away Number and Contact Information.

5. Blank Basketball Court Templates - Write your plays, drills, etc.

6. Statistics At A Glance Pages - 39 Games, Including: Points, Rebounds, Assists, Steals, Blocks, Turnovers, Fouls and Total Points.

7. Notes - Includes ample pages of blank lined notes for any other extra or important info you would like to write.

Enjoy!

Month Of: _____

SUN	MON	TUES	WED	THURS	FRI	SAT

Month Of:_____

SUN	MON	TUES	WED	THURS	FRI	SAT

Month Of:_____

SUN	MON	TUES	WED	THURS	FRI	SAT

Month Of: _____

SUN	MON	TUES	WED	THURS	FRI	SAT

Month Of: _____

SUN	MON	TUES	WED	THURS	FRI	SAT

Month Of:_____

SUN	MON	TUES	WED	THURS	FRI	SAT

Month Of: _____

SUN	MON	TUES	WED	THURS	FRI	SAT

Month Of:_____

SUN	MON	TUES	WED	THURS	FRI	SAT

Month Of: _____

SUN	MON	TUES	WED	THURS	FRI	SAT

Month Of:_____

SUN	MON	TUES	WED	THURS	FRI	SAT

Month Of:_____

SUN	MON	TUES	WED	THURS	FRI	SAT

Month Of:_____

SUN	MON	TUES	WED	THURS	FRI	SAT

Index of Games

1. _____   _____   _____   _____   _____
   Opponent   Date   Location   W/L   Score

2. _____   _____   _____   _____   _____
   Opponent   Date   Location   W/L   Score

3. _____   _____   _____   _____   _____
   Opponent   Date   Location   W/L   Score

4. _____   _____   _____   _____   _____
   Opponent   Date   Location   W/L   Score

5. _____   _____   _____   _____   _____
   Opponent   Date   Location   W/L   Score

6. _____   _____   _____   _____   _____
   Opponent   Date   Location   W/L   Score

7. _____   _____   _____   _____   _____
   Opponent   Date   Location   W/L   Score

8. _____   _____   _____   _____   _____
   Opponent   Date   Location   W/L   Score

Index of Games

9	_____ Opponent	_____ Date	_____ Location	_____ W/L	_____ Score
10	_____ Opponent	_____ Date	_____ Location	_____ W/L	_____ Score
11	_____ Opponent	_____ Date	_____ Location	_____ W/L	_____ Score
12	_____ Opponent	_____ Date	_____ Location	_____ W/L	_____ Score
13	_____ Opponent	_____ Date	_____ Location	_____ W/L	_____ Score
14	_____ Opponent	_____ Date	_____ Location	_____ W/L	_____ Score
15	_____ Opponent	_____ Date	_____ Location	_____ W/L	_____ Score
16	_____ Opponent	_____ Date	_____ Location	_____ W/L	_____ Score

Index of Games

17 _____	_____	_____	_____	_____
Opponent	Date	Location	W/L	Score

18 _____	_____	_____	_____	_____
Opponent	Date	Location	W/L	Score

19 _____	_____	_____	_____	_____
Opponent	Date	Location	W/L	Score

20 _____	_____	_____	_____	_____
Opponent	Date	Location	W/L	Score

21 _____	_____	_____	_____	_____
Opponent	Date	Location	W/L	Score

22 _____	_____	_____	_____	_____
Opponent	Date	Location	W/L	Score

23 _____	_____	_____	_____	_____
Opponent	Date	Location	W/L	Score

24 _____	_____	_____	_____	_____
Opponent	Date	Location	W/L	Score

Index of Games

25	_____	_____	_____	_____	_____
	Opponent	Date	Location	W/L	Score

26	_____	_____	_____	_____	_____
	Opponent	Date	Location	W/L	Score

27	_____	_____	_____	_____	_____
	Opponent	Date	Location	W/L	Score

28	_____	_____	_____	_____	_____
	Opponent	Date	Location	W/L	Score

29	_____	_____	_____	_____	_____
	Opponent	Date	Location	W/L	Score

30	_____	_____	_____	_____	_____
	Opponent	Date	Location	W/L	Score

31	_____	_____	_____	_____	_____
	Opponent	Date	Location	W/L	Score

32	_____	_____	_____	_____	_____
	Opponent	Date	Location	W/L	Score

Index of Games

33	_____	_____	_____	_____	_____
	Opponent	Date	Location	W/L	Score

34	_____	_____	_____	_____	_____
	Opponent	Date	Location	W/L	Score

35	_____	_____	_____	_____	_____
	Opponent	Date	Location	W/L	Score

36	_____	_____	_____	_____	_____
	Opponent	Date	Location	W/L	Score

37	_____	_____	_____	_____	_____
	Opponent	Date	Location	W/L	Score

38	_____	_____	_____	_____	_____
	Opponent	Date	Location	W/L	Score

39	_____	_____	_____	_____	_____
	Opponent	Date	Location	W/L	Score

40	_____	_____	_____	_____	_____
	Opponent	Date	Location	W/L	Score

Player Roster

HOME #	AWAY #	LAST NAME	FIRST NAME	YEAR	EMERGENCY CONTACT

Player Roster

HOME #	AWAY #	LAST NAME	FIRST NAME	YEAR	EMERGENCY CONTACT

Play Name:_____

Play Name:_____

Play Name:_____

Play Name:_____

Play Name:_____

Play Name:_____

Play Name:_____

Play Name:_____

Play Name:_____

Play Name:_____

Play Name:_____

Play Name:_____

Play Name:_____

Play Name:_____

Play Name:_____

Play Name:_____

_____
_____
_____
_____
_____
_____
_____

Play Name:_____

Play Name:_____

Play Name:_____

Play Name:_____

Statistics At A Glance

Date:_____   Opponent:_____   Home/Away

Player	#	Points	Rebounds	Assists	Steals	Blocks	Turnovers	Fouls	Total Points

Score

Halftime: Us_____ Them_____   Final: Us_____ Them_____

Statistics At A Glance

Date:_____   Opponent:_____   Home/Away

Player	#	Points	Rebounds	Assists	Steals	Blocks	Turnovers	Fouls	Total Points

Score

Halftime: Us_____ Them_____   Final: Us_____ Them_____

Statistics At A Glance

Date:_____   Opponent:_____   Home/Away

Player	#	Points	Rebounds	Assists	Steals	Blocks	Turnovers	Fouls	Total Points

Score

Halftime: Us_____   Them_____   Final: Us_____   Them_____

Statistics At A Glance

Date:_____ Opponent:_____ Home/Away

Player	#	Points	Rebounds	Assists	Steals	Blocks	Turnovers	Fouls	Total Points

Score

Halftime: Us_____ Them_____   Final: Us_____ Them_____

Statistics At A Glance

Date:_____ Opponent:_____ Home/Away

Player	#	Points	Rebounds	Assists	Steals	Blocks	Turnovers	Fouls	Total Points

Score

Halftime: Us_____ Them_____   Final: Us_____ Them_____

Statistics At A Glance

Date:_____   Opponent:_____   Home/Away

Player	#	Points	Rebounds	Assists	Steals	Blocks	Turnovers	Fouls	Total Points

Score

Halftime: Us_____   Them_____   Final: Us_____   Them_____

Statistics At A Glance

Date:_____   Opponent:_____   Home/Away

Player	#	Points	Rebounds	Assists	Steals	Blocks	Turnovers	Fouls	Total Points

Score

Halftime: Us_____   Them_____   Final: Us_____   Them_____

Statistics At A Glance

Date:_____   Opponent:_____   Home/Away

Player	#	Points	Rebounds	Assists	Steals	Blocks	Turnovers	Fouls	Total Points

Score

Halftime: Us_____   Them_____   Final: Us_____   Them_____

Statistics At A Glance

Date:_____ Opponent:_____ Home/Away

Player	#	Points	Rebounds	Assists	Steals	Blocks	Turnovers	Fouls	Total Points

Score

Halftime: Us_____ Them_____   Final: Us_____ Them_____

Statistics At A Glance

Date:_____   Opponent:_____   Home/Away

Player	#	Points	Rebounds	Assists	Steals	Blocks	Turnovers	Fouls	Total Points

Score

Halftime: Us_____   Them_____   Final: Us_____   Them_____

Statistics At A Glance

Date:_____ Opponent:_____ Home/Away

Player	#	Points	Rebounds	Assists	Steals	Blocks	Turnovers	Fouls	Total Points

Score

Halftime: Us_____ Them_____   Final: Us_____ Them_____

Statistics At A Glance

Date:_____ Opponent:_____ Home/Away

Player	#	Points	Rebounds	Assists	Steals	Blocks	Turnovers	Fouls	Total Points

Score

Halftime: Us_____ Them_____   Final: Us_____ Them_____

Statistics At A Glance

Date:_____ Opponent:_____ Home/Away

Player	#	Points	Rebounds	Assists	Steals	Blocks	Turnovers	Fouls	Total Points

Score

Halftime: Us_____ Them_____   Final: Us_____ Them_____

Statistics At A Glance

Date:_____   Opponent:_____   Home/Away

Player	#	Points	Rebounds	Assists	Steals	Blocks	Turnovers	Fouls	Total Points

Score

Halftime: Us_____ Them_____   Final: Us_____ Them_____

Statistics At A Glance

Date:_____   Opponent:_____   Home/Away

Player	#	Points	Rebounds	Assists	Steals	Blocks	Turnovers	Fouls	Total Points

Score

Halftime: Us_____ Them_____   Final: Us_____ Them_____

Statistics At A Glance

Date:_____   Opponent:_____   Home/Away

Player	#	Points	Rebounds	Assists	Steals	Blocks	Turnovers	Fouls	Total Points

Score

Halftime: Us_____ Them_____   Final: Us_____ Them_____

Statistics At A Glance

Date:_____   Opponent:_____   Home/Away

Player	#	Points	Rebounds	Assists	Steals	Blocks	Turnovers	Fouls	Total Points

Score

Halftime: Us_____ Them_____   Final: Us_____ Them_____

Statistics At A Glance

Date:_____   Opponent:_____   Home/Away

Player	#	Points	Rebounds	Assists	Steals	Blocks	Turnovers	Fouls	Total Points

Score

Halftime: Us_____   Them_____   Final: Us_____   Them_____

Statistics At A Glance

Date:_____ Opponent:_____ Home/Away

Player	#	Points	Rebounds	Assists	Steals	Blocks	Turnovers	Fouls	Total Points

Score

Halftime: Us_____ Them_____   Final: Us_____ Them_____

Statistics At A Glance

Date:_____   Opponent:_____   Home/Away

Player	#	Points	Rebounds	Assists	Steals	Blocks	Turnovers	Fouls	Total Points

Score

Halftime: Us_____   Them_____   Final: Us_____   Them_____

Statistics At A Glance

Date:_____   Opponent:_____   Home/Away

Player	#	Points	Rebounds	Assists	Steals	Blocks	Turnovers	Fouls	Total Points

Score

Halftime: Us_____ Them_____   Final: Us_____ Them_____

Statistics At A Glance

Date:_____   Opponent:_____   Home/Away

Player	#	Points	Rebounds	Assists	Steals	Blocks	Turnovers	Fouls	Total Points

Score

Halftime: Us_____ Them_____   Final: Us_____ Them_____

Statistics At A Glance

Date:_____ Opponent:_____ Home/Away

Player	#	Points	Rebounds	Assists	Steals	Blocks	Turnovers	Fouls	Total Points

Score

Halftime: Us_____ Them_____   Final: Us_____ Them_____

Statistics At A Glance

Date:_____   Opponent:_____   Home/Away

Player	#	Points	Rebounds	Assists	Steals	Blocks	Turnovers	Fouls	Total Points

Score

Halftime: Us_____ Them_____   Final: Us_____ Them_____

Statistics At A Glance

Date:_____ Opponent:_____ Home/Away

Player	#	Points	Rebounds	Assists	Steals	Blocks	Turnovers	Fouls	Total Points

Score

Halftime: Us_____ Them_____ Final: Us_____ Them_____

Statistics At A Glance

Date:_____   Opponent:_____   Home/Away

Player	#	Points	Rebounds	Assists	Steals	Blocks	Turnovers	Fouls	Total Points

Score

Halftime: Us_____ Them_____   Final: Us_____ Them_____

Statistics At A Glance

Date:_____   Opponent:_____   Home/Away

Player	#	Points	Rebounds	Assists	Steals	Blocks	Turnovers	Fouls	Total Points

Score

Halftime: Us_____ Them_____   Final: Us_____ Them_____

Statistics At A Glance

Date:_____ Opponent:_____ Home/Away

Player	#	Points	Rebounds	Assists	Steals	Blocks	Turnovers	Fouls	Total Points

Score

Halftime: Us_____ Them_____   Final: Us_____ Them_____

Statistics At A Glance

Date:_____   Opponent:_____   Home/Away

Player	#	Points	Rebounds	Assists	Steals	Blocks	Turnovers	Fouls	Total Points

Score

Halftime: Us_____ Them_____   Final: Us_____ Them_____

Statistics At A Glance

Date:_____   Opponent:_____   Home/Away

Player	#	Points	Rebounds	Assists	Steals	Blocks	Turnovers	Fouls	Total Points

Score

Halftime: Us_____ Them_____   Final: Us_____ Them_____

Statistics At A Glance

Date:_____ Opponent:_____ Home/Away

Player	#	Points	Rebounds	Assists	Steals	Blocks	Turnovers	Fouls	Total Points

Score

Halftime: Us_____ Them_____ Final: Us_____ Them_____

Statistics At A Glance

Date:_____ Opponent:_____ Home/Away

Player	#	Points	Rebounds	Assists	Steals	Blocks	Turnovers	Fouls	Total Points

Score

Halftime: Us_____ Them_____ Final: Us_____ Them_____

Statistics At A Glance

Date:_____　　　Opponent:_____　　　Home/Away

Player	#	Points	Rebounds	Assists	Steals	Blocks	Turnovers	Fouls	Total Points

Score

Halftime: Us_____　Them_____　　　　Final: Us_____　Them_____

Statistics At A Glance

Date:_____   Opponent:_____   Home/Away

Player	#	Points	Rebounds	Assists	Steals	Blocks	Turnovers	Fouls	Total Points

Score

Halftime: Us_____ Them_____   Final: Us_____ Them_____

Statistics At A Glance

Date:_____ Opponent:_____ Home/Away

Player	#	Points	Rebounds	Assists	Steals	Blocks	Turnovers	Fouls	Total Points

Score

Halftime: Us_____ Them_____ Final: Us_____ Them_____

Statistics At A Glance

Date:_____ Opponent:_____ Home/Away

Player	#	Points	Rebounds	Assists	Steals	Blocks	Turnovers	Fouls	Total Points

Score

Halftime: Us_____ Them_____   Final: Us_____ Them_____

Statistics At A Glance

Date:_____ Opponent:_____ Home/Away

Player	#	Points	Rebounds	Assists	Steals	Blocks	Turnovers	Fouls	Total Points

Score

Halftime: Us_____ Them_____   Final: Us_____ Them_____

Statistics At A Glance

Date:_____   Opponent:_____   Home/Away

Player	#	Points	Rebounds	Assists	Steals	Blocks	Turnovers	Fouls	Total Points

Score

Halftime: Us_____   Them_____   Final: Us_____   Them_____

Statistics At A Glance

Date:_____ Opponent:_____ Home/Away

Player	#	Points	Rebounds	Assists	Steals	Blocks	Turnovers	Fouls	Total Points

Score

Halftime: Us_____ Them_____   Final: Us_____ Them_____

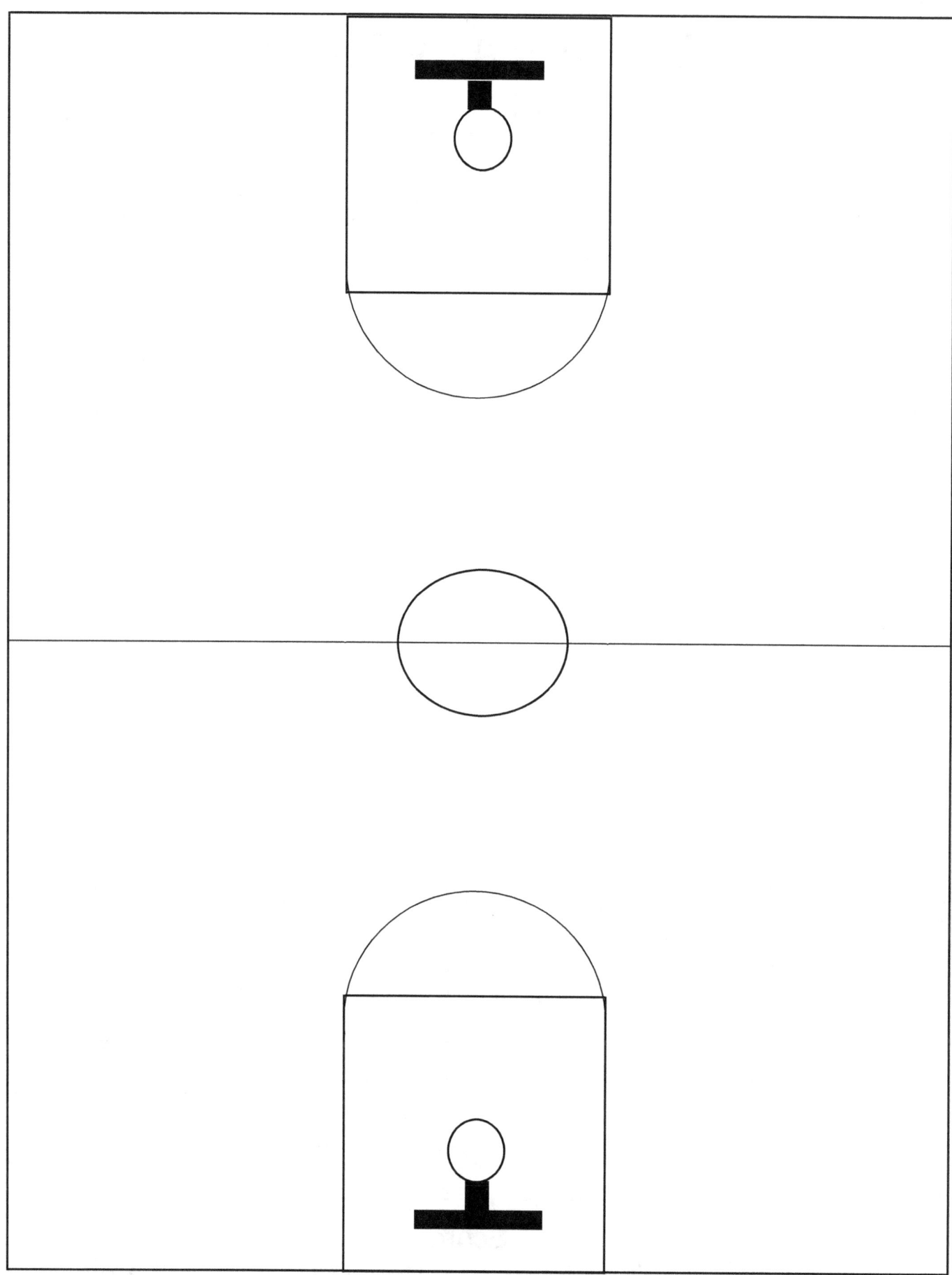

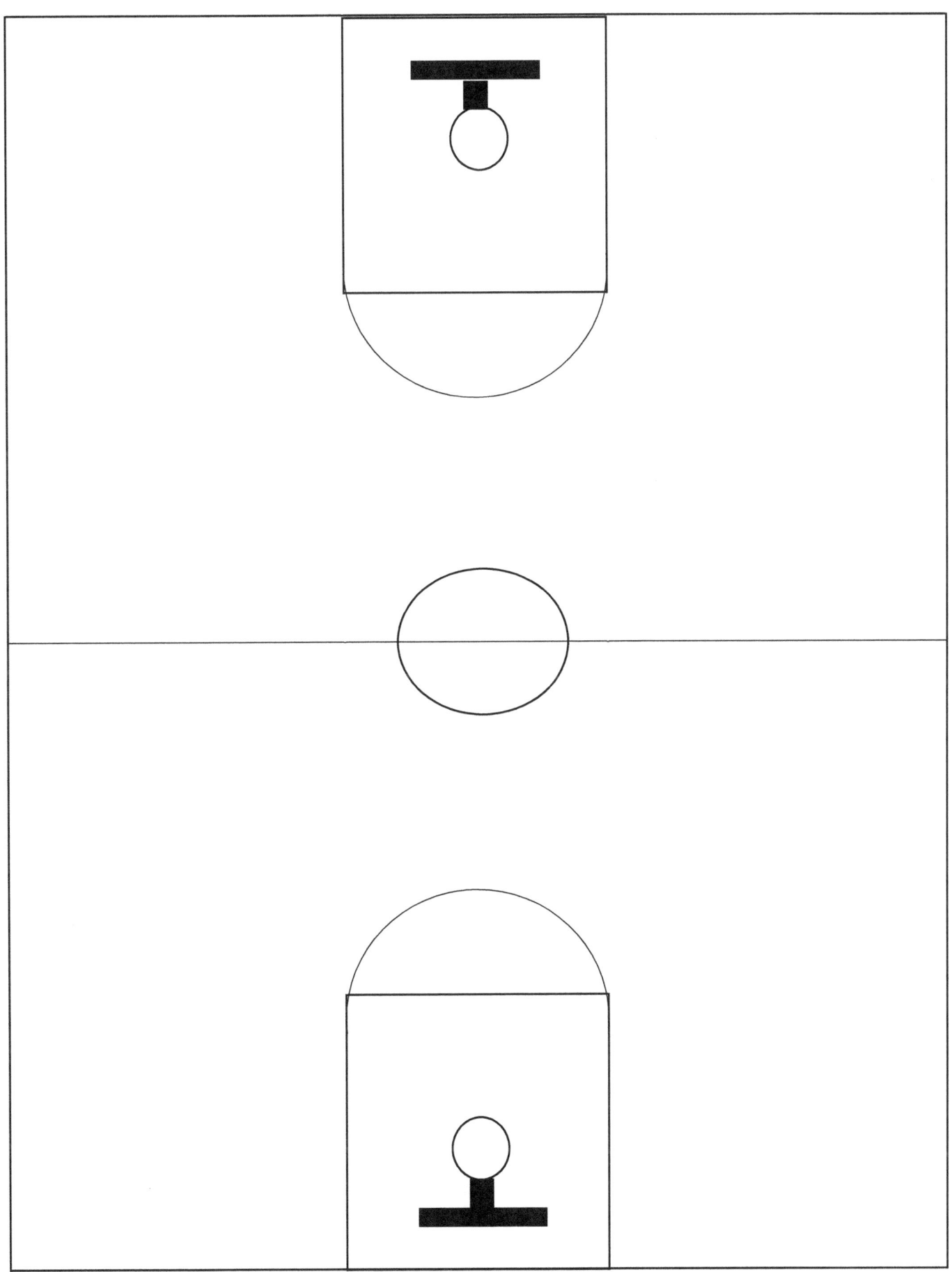

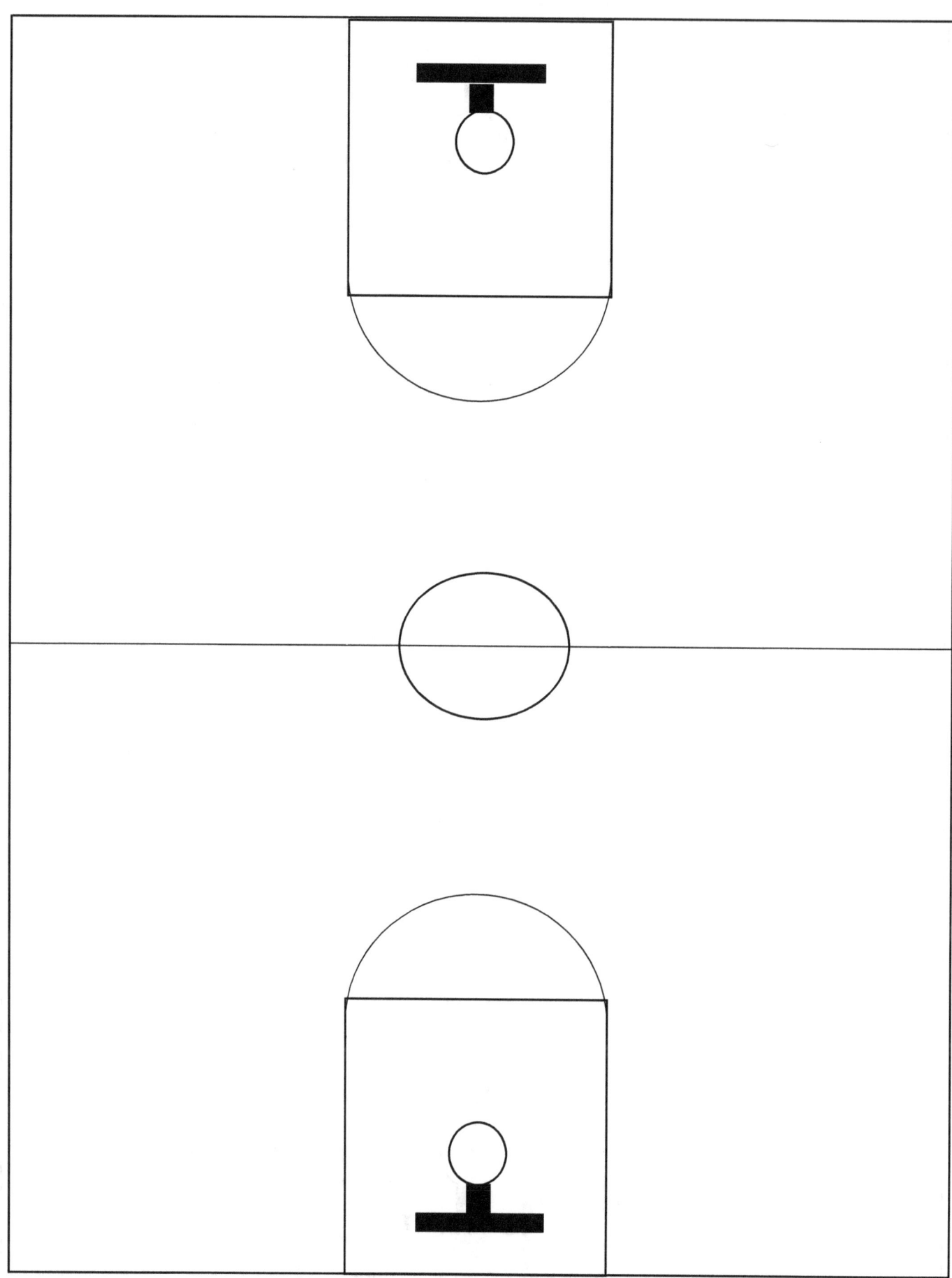

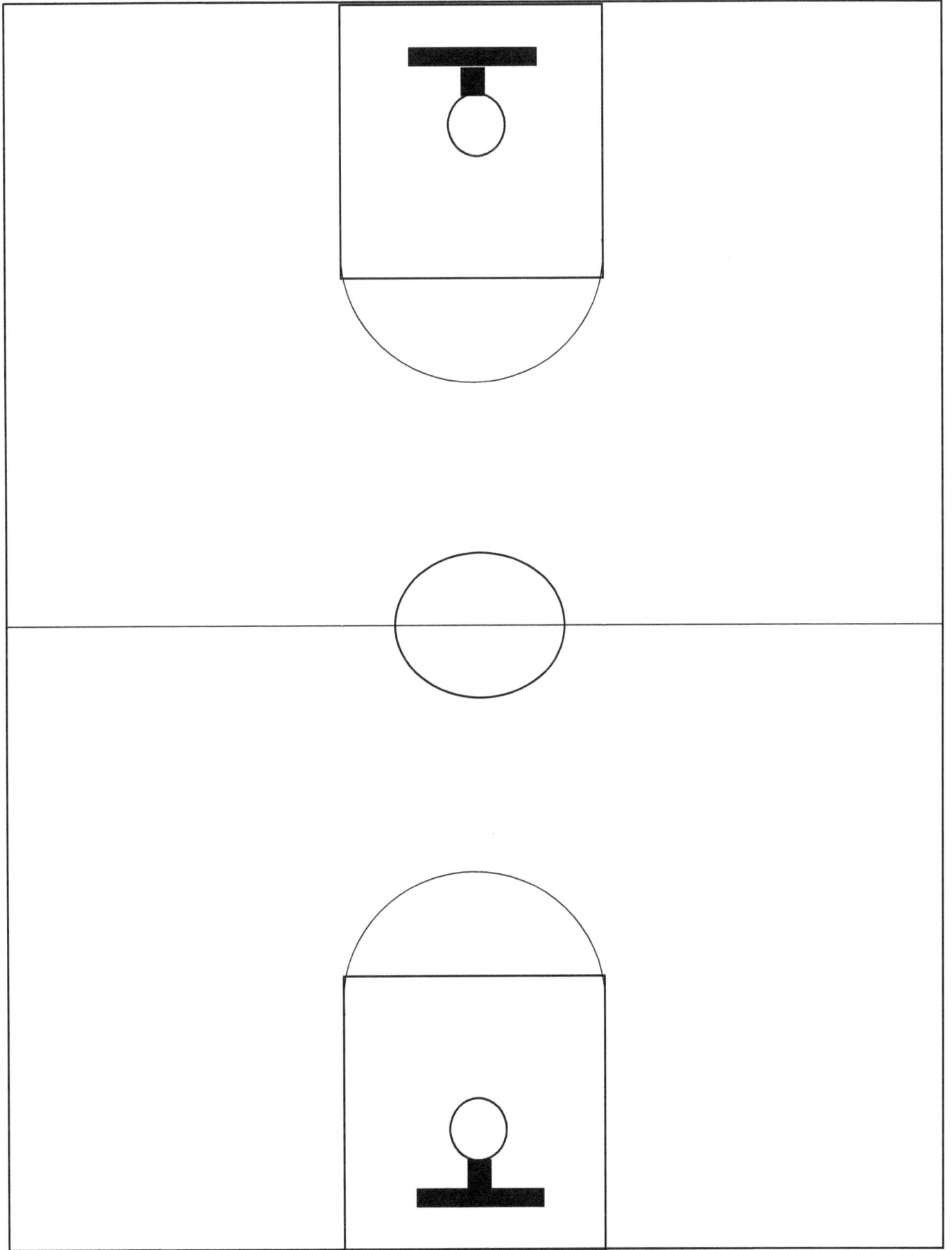

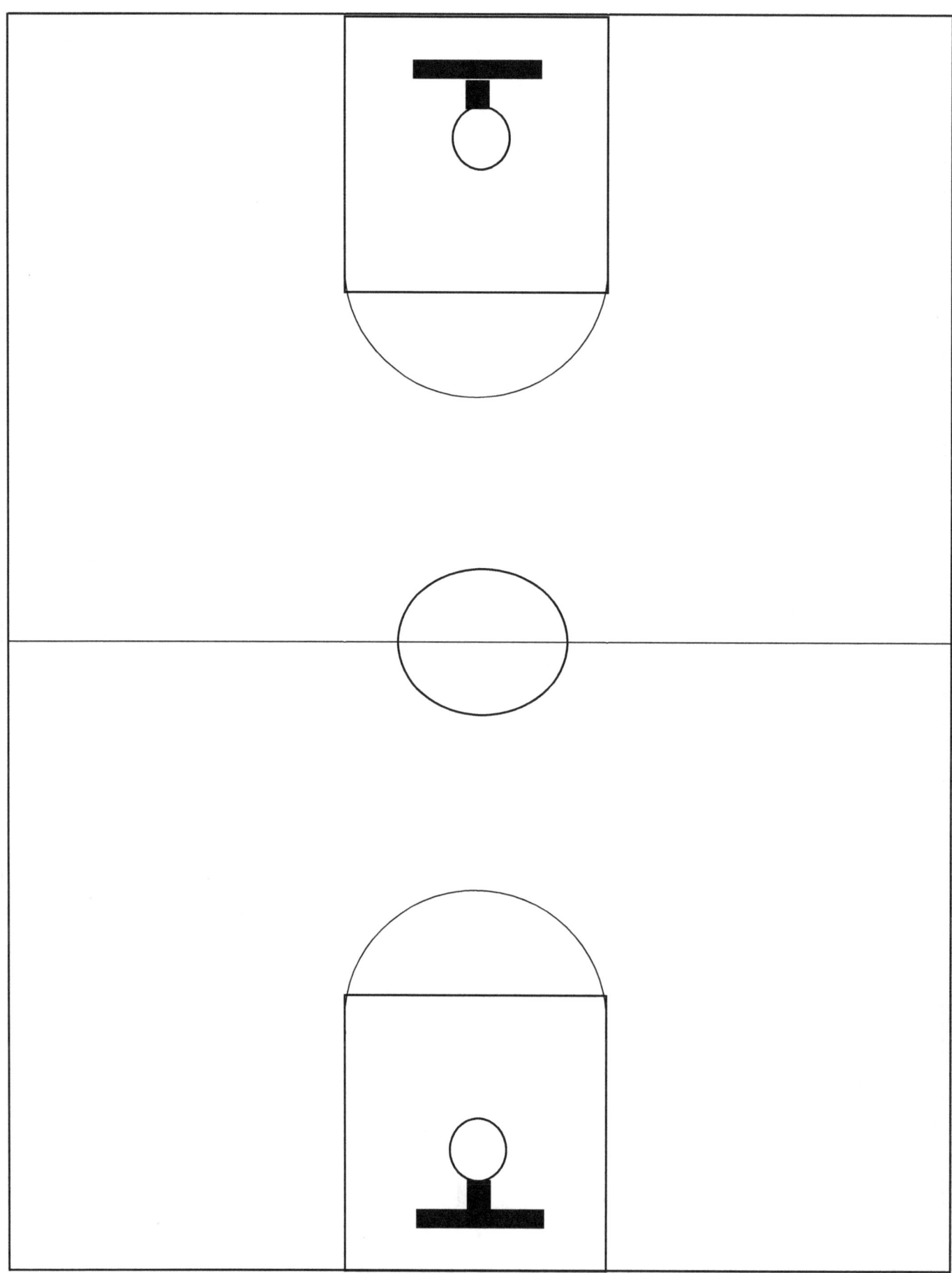

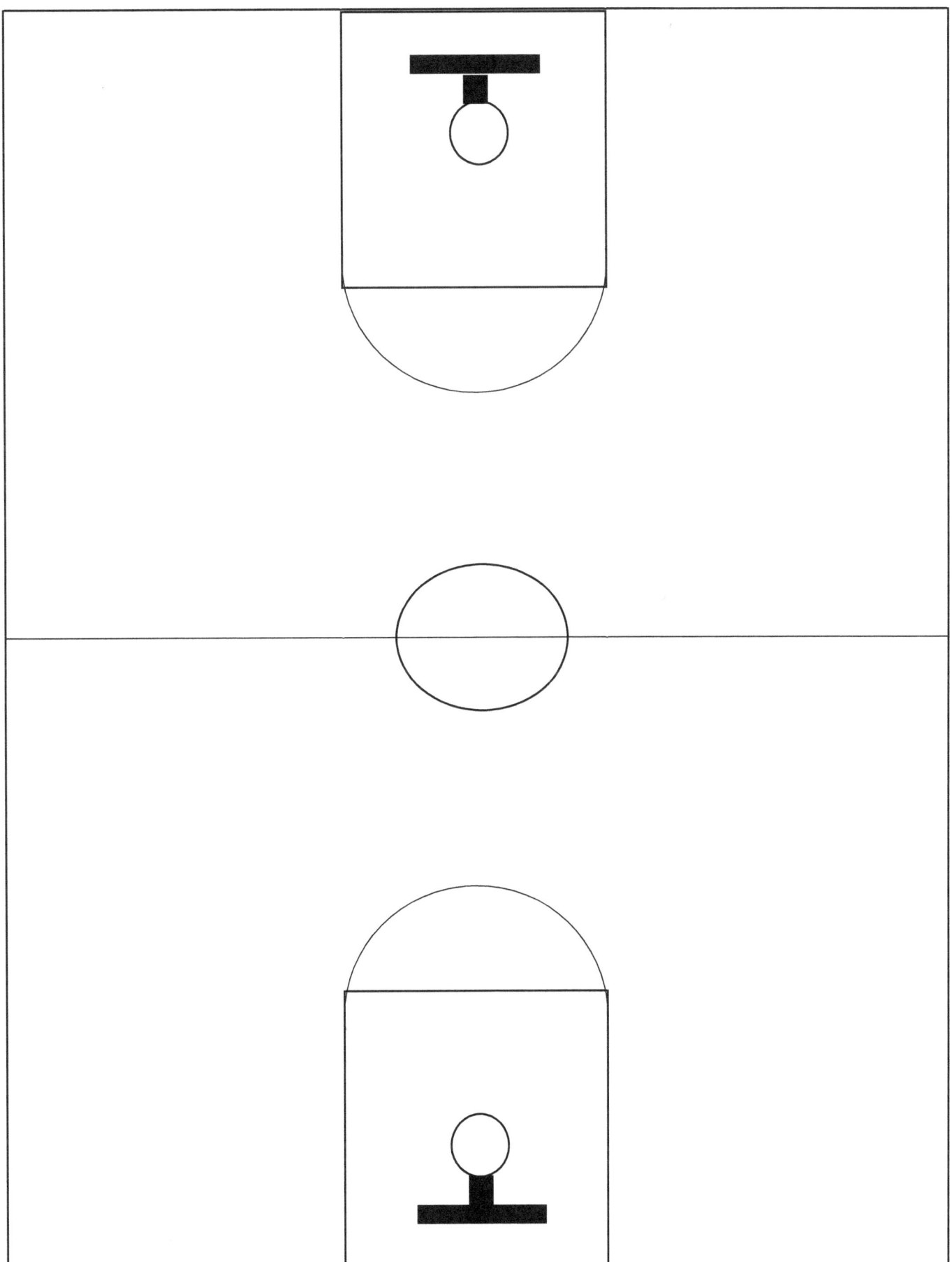

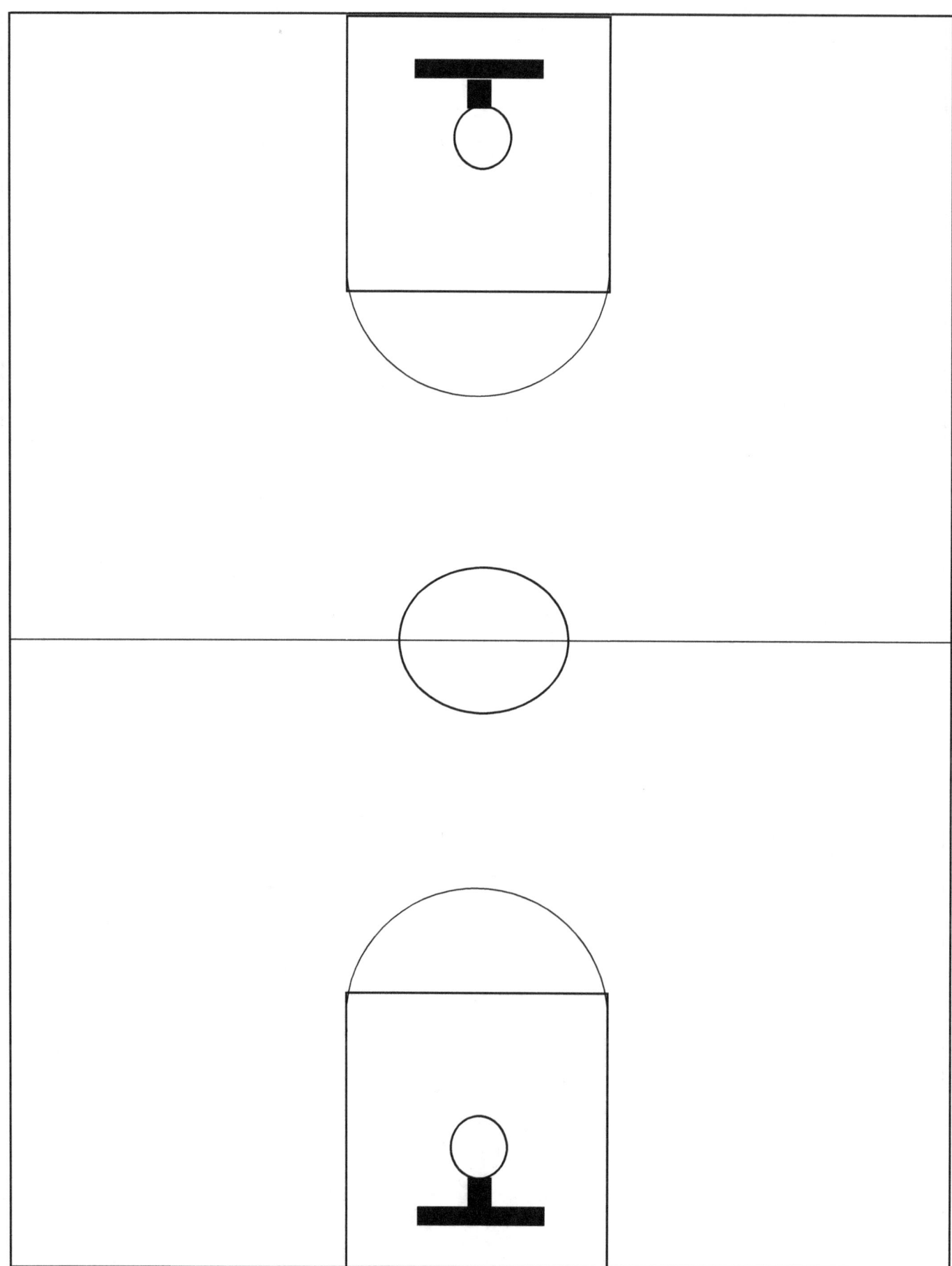

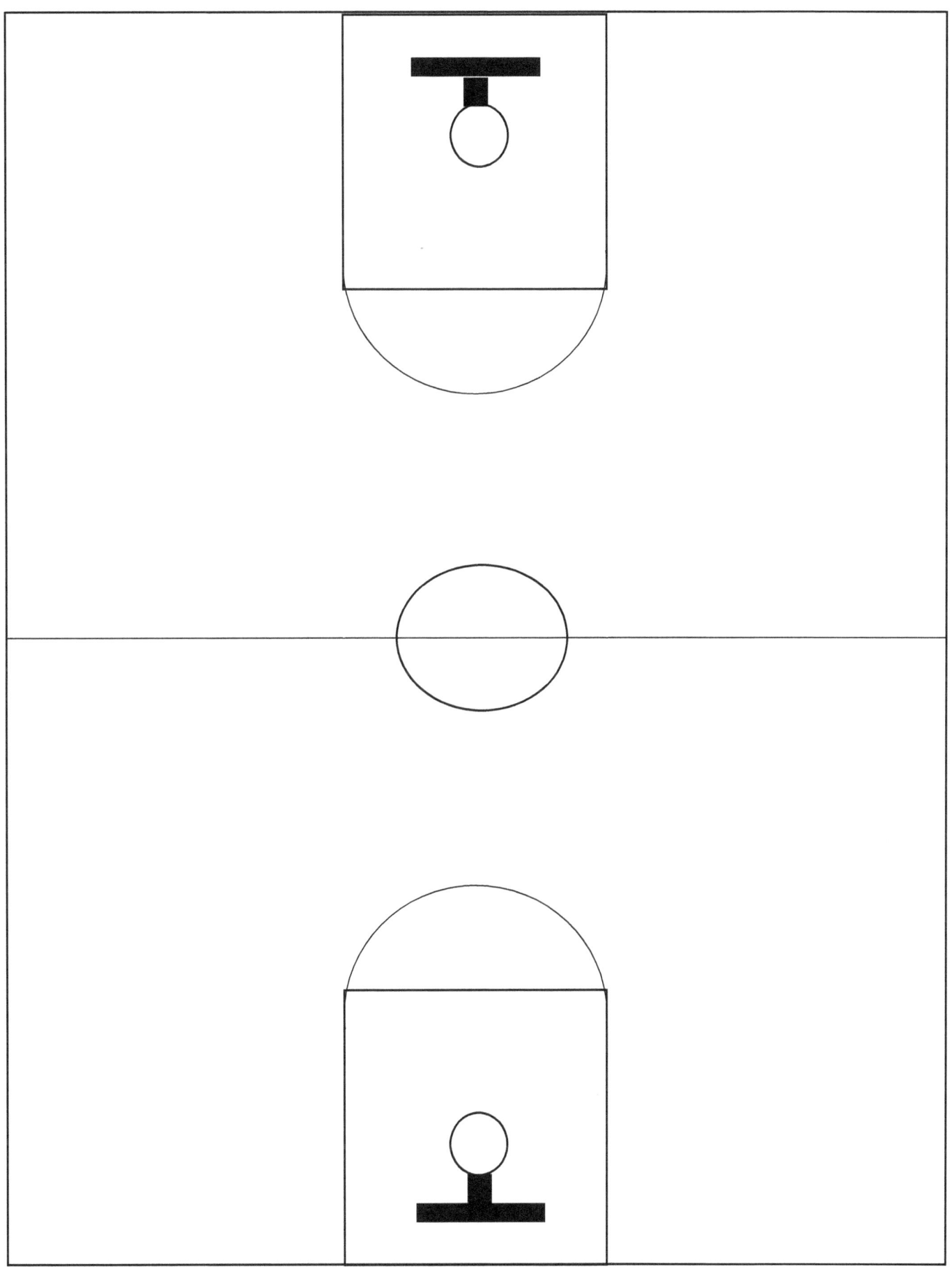

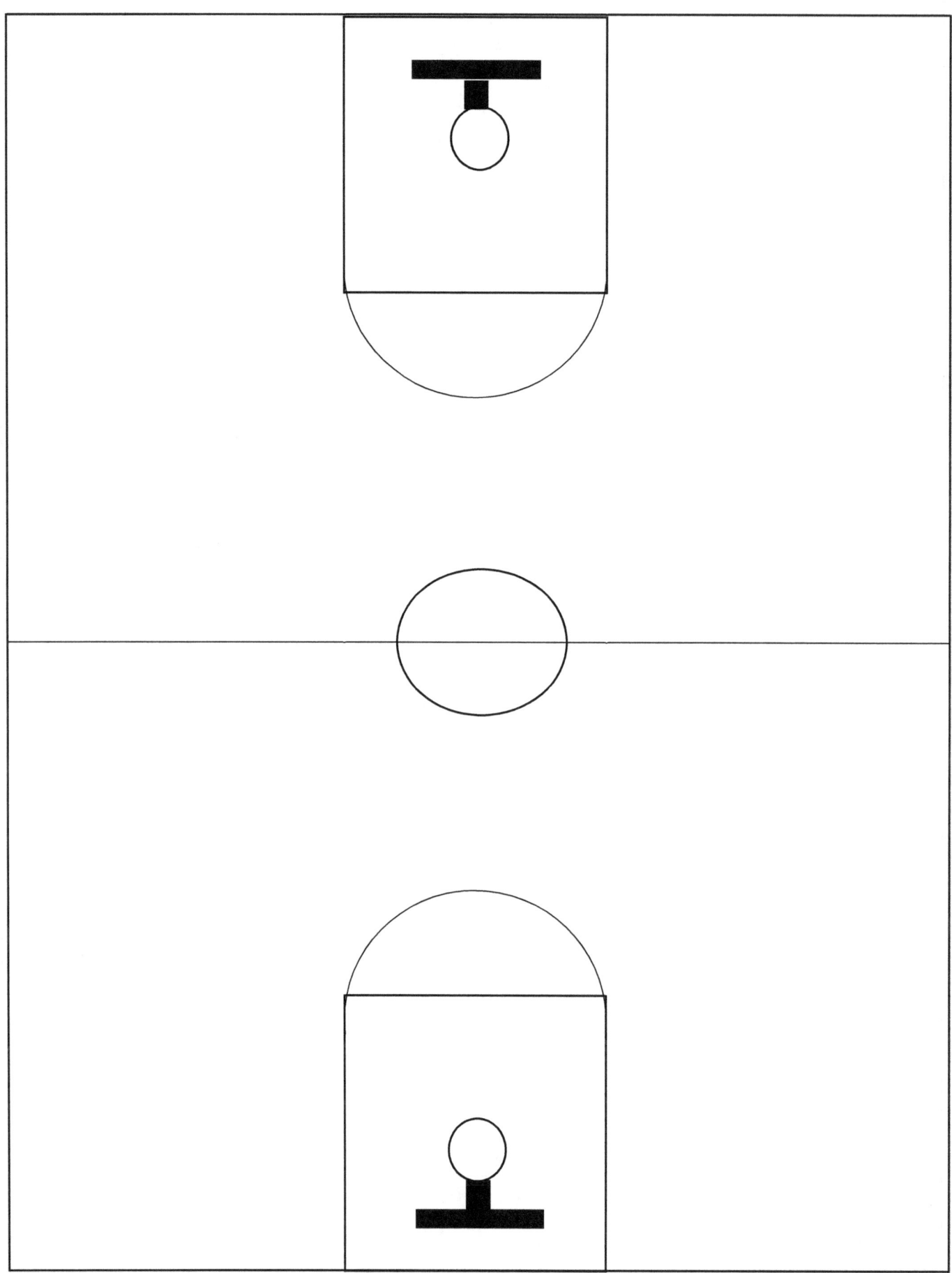

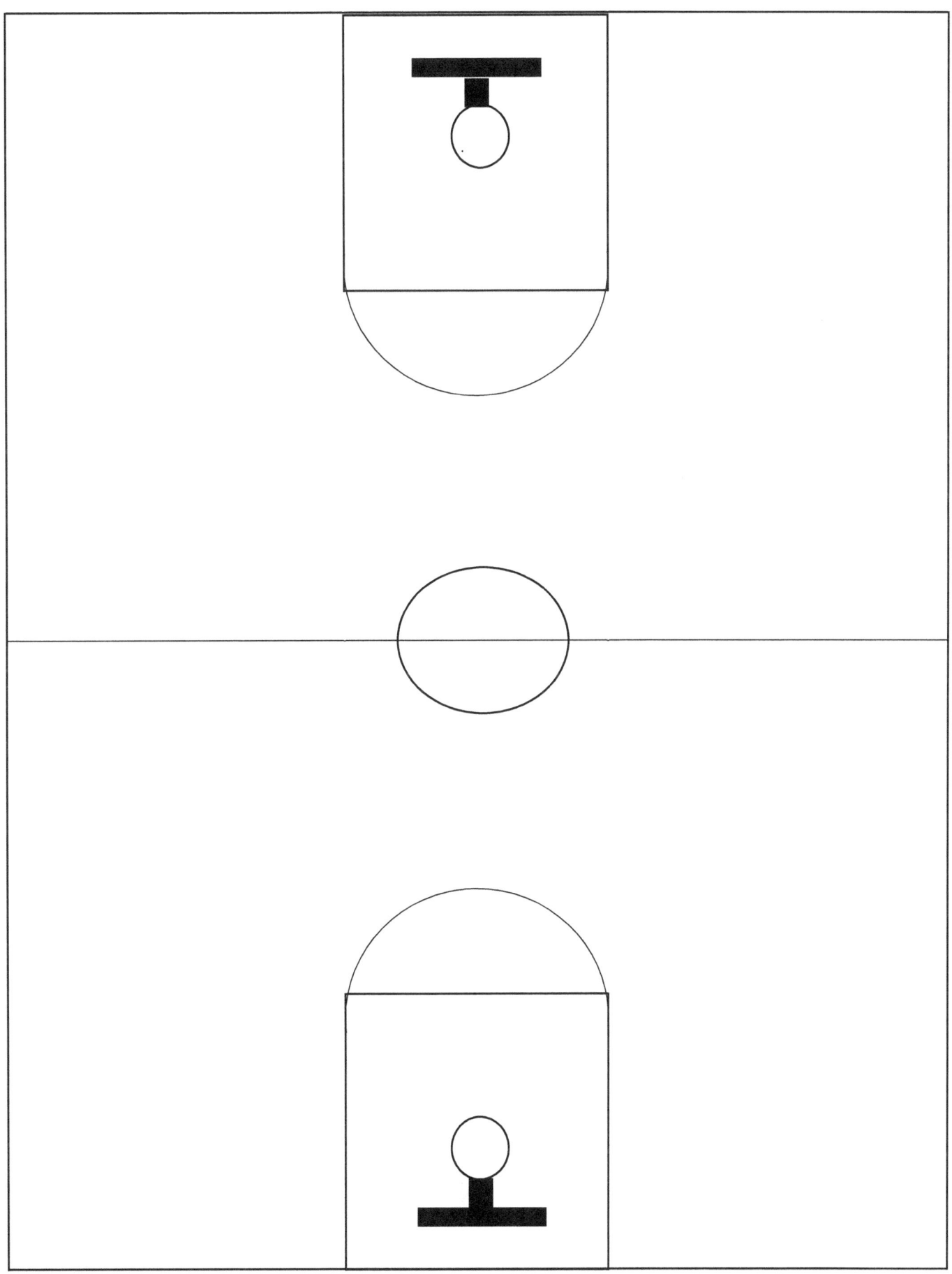

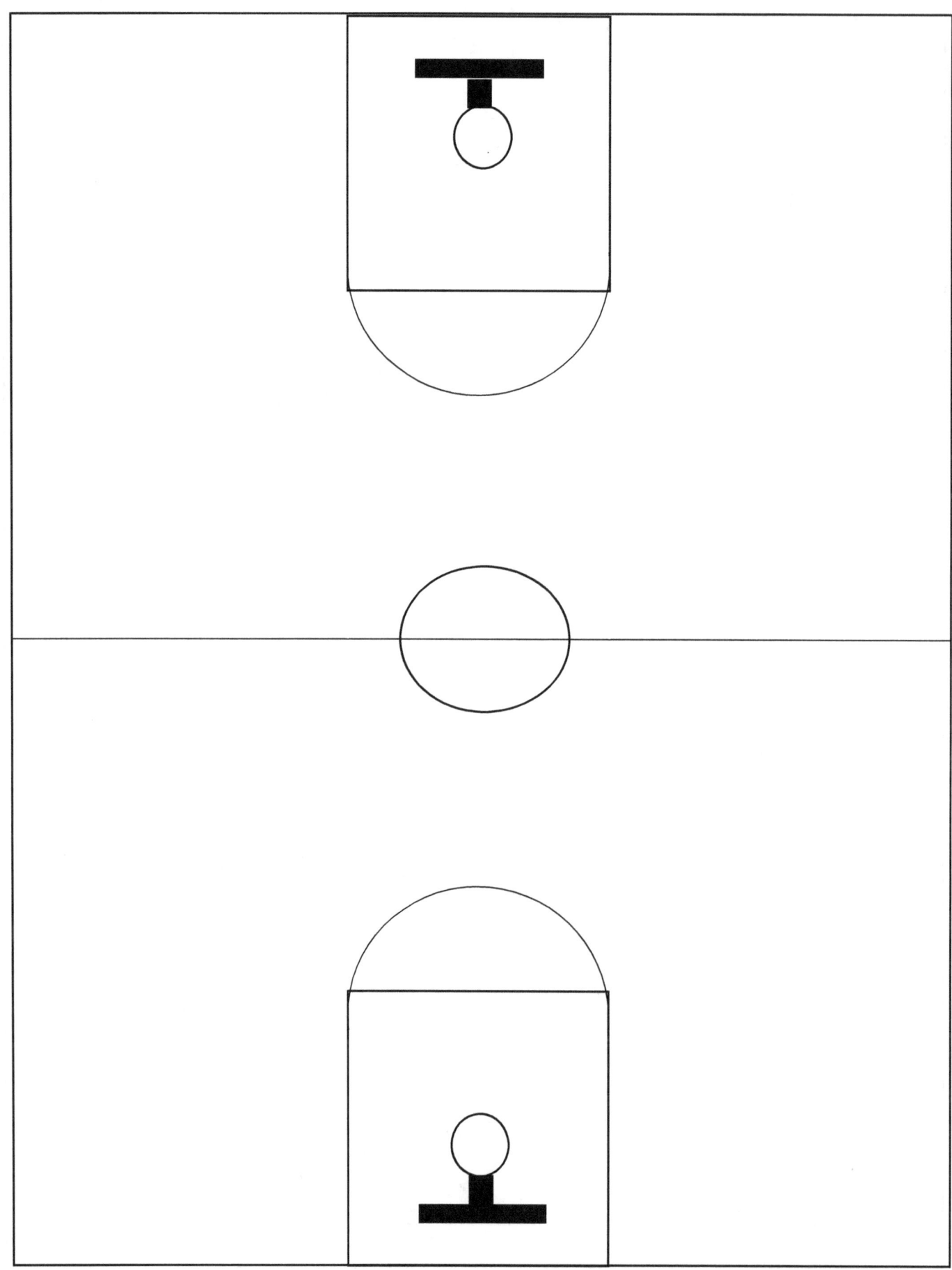

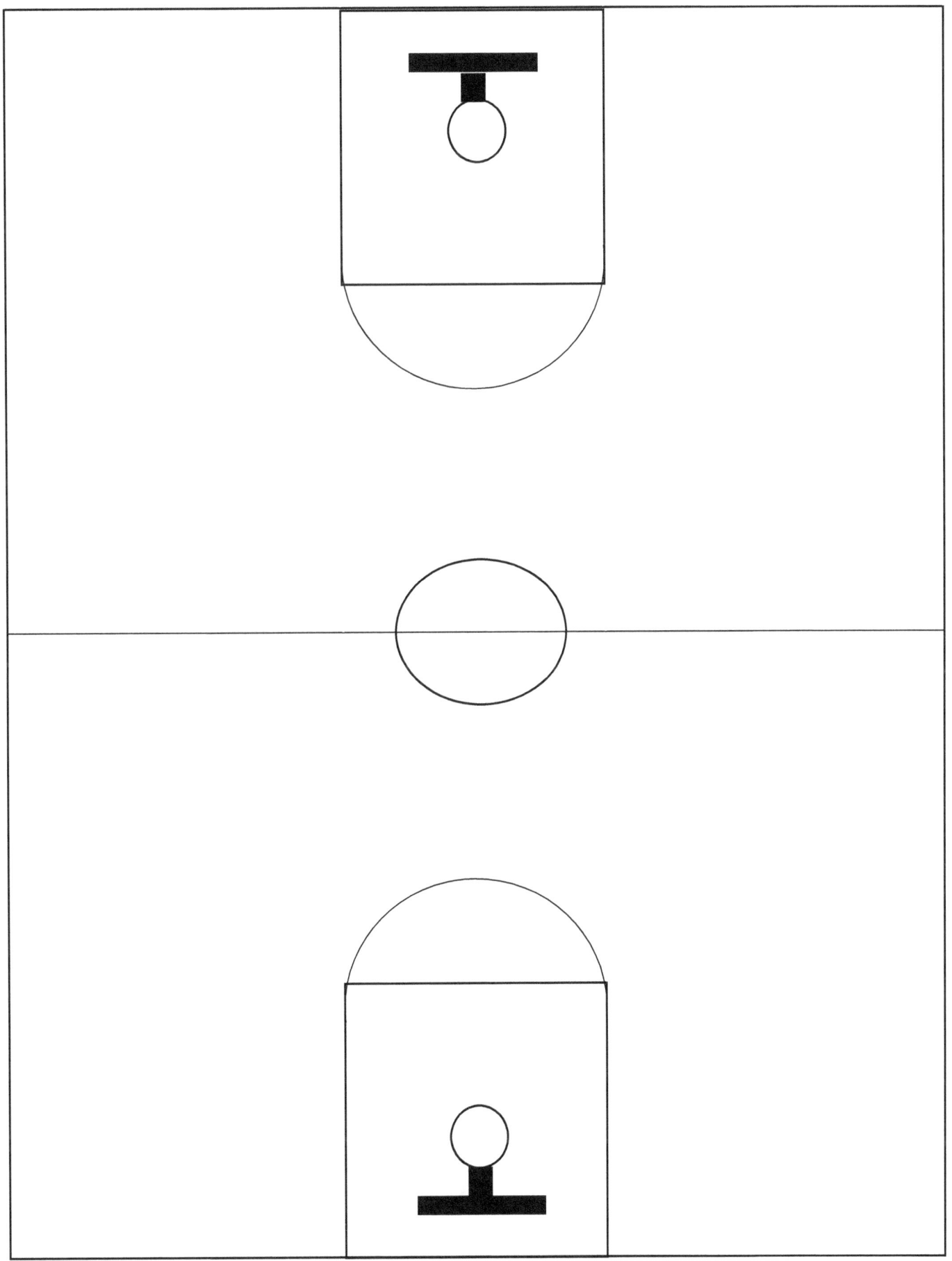

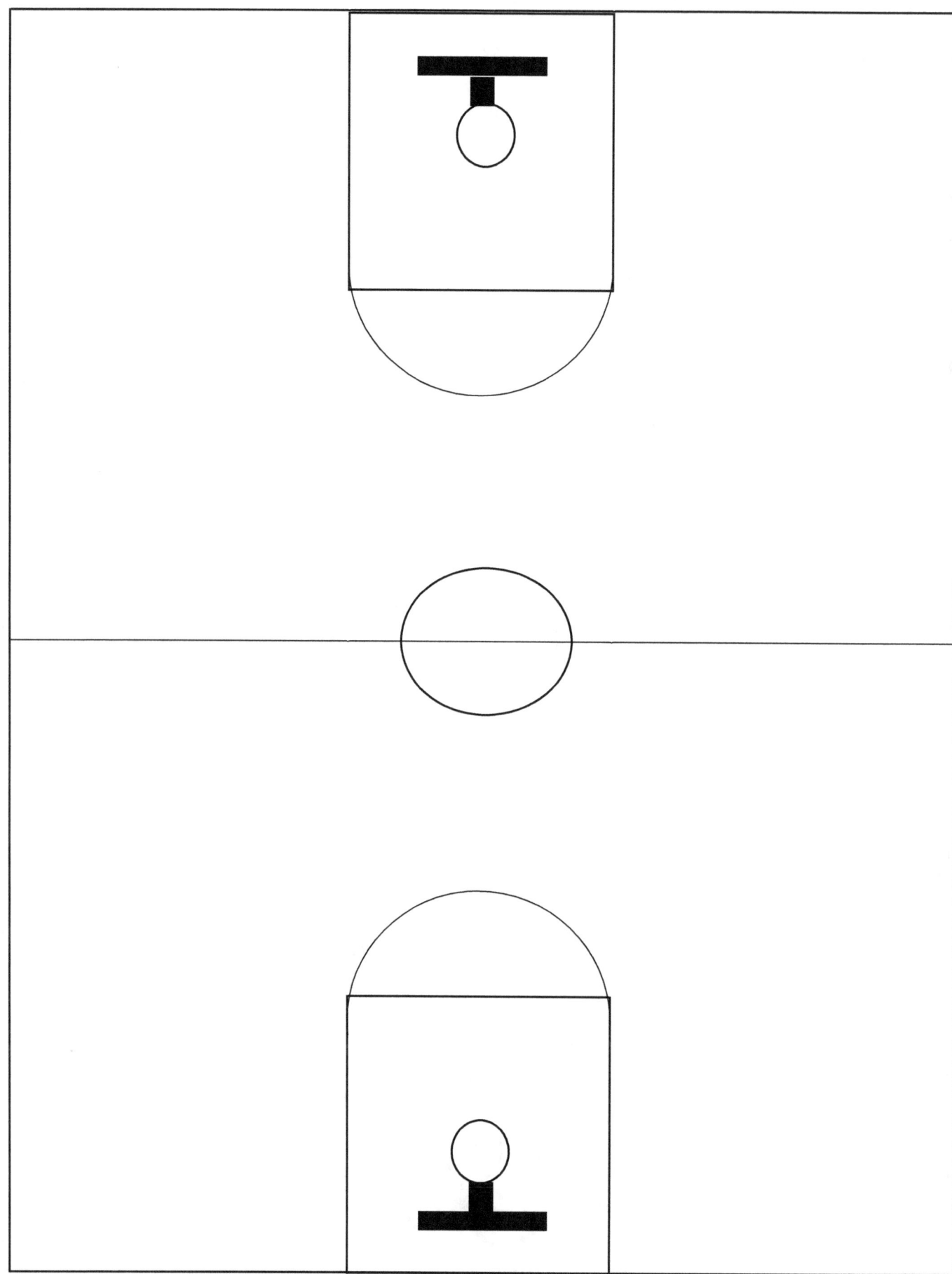

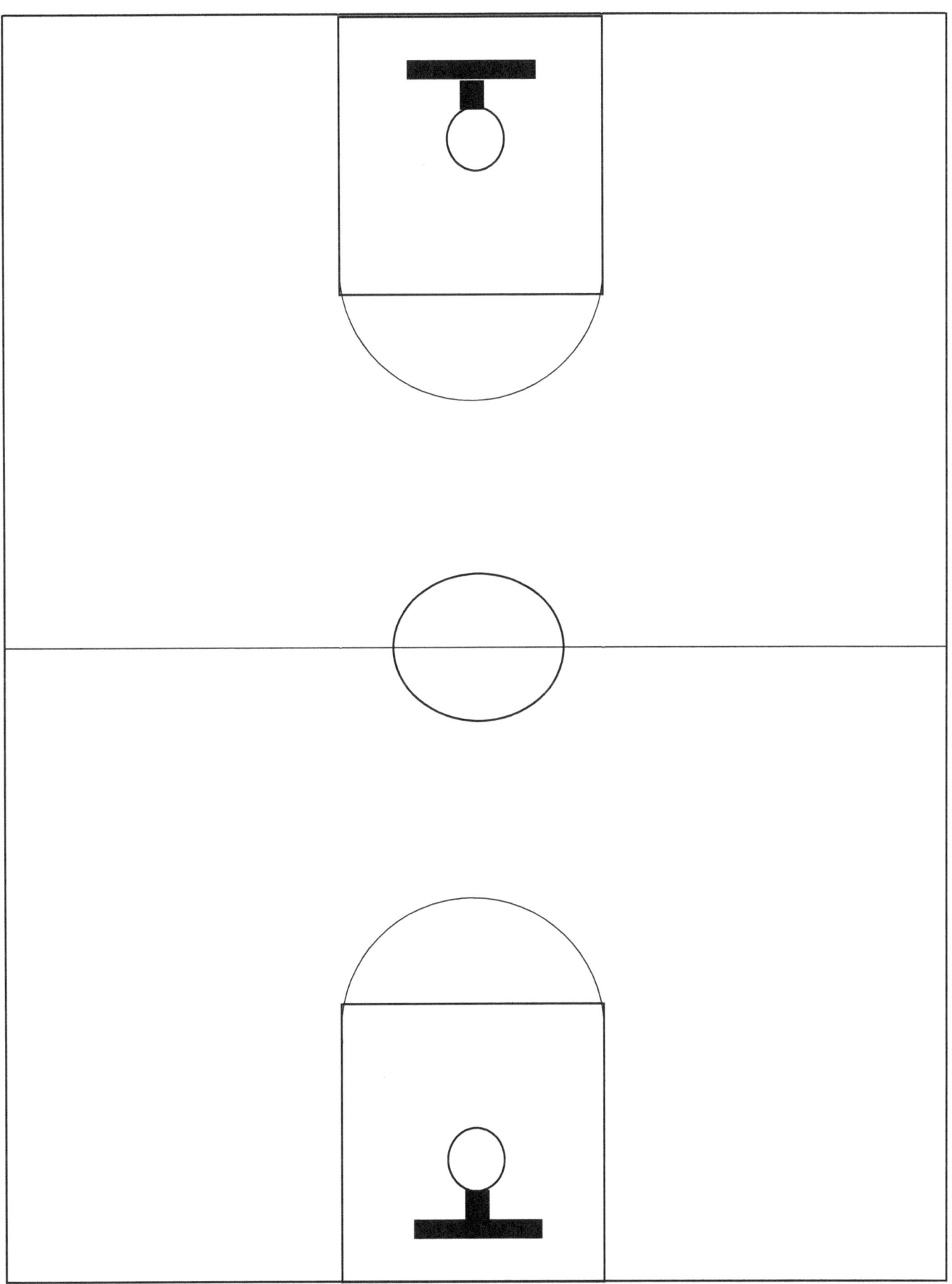

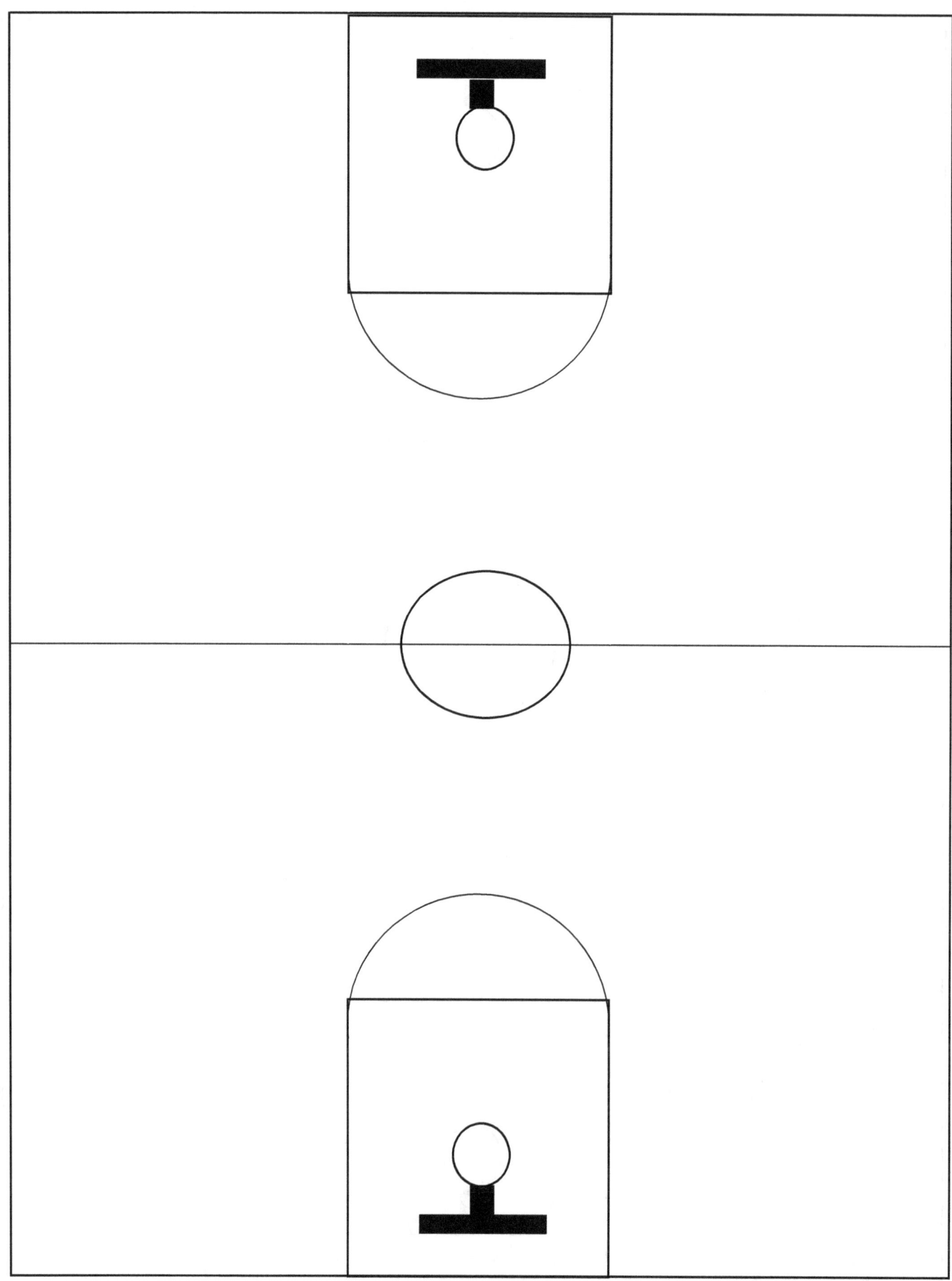

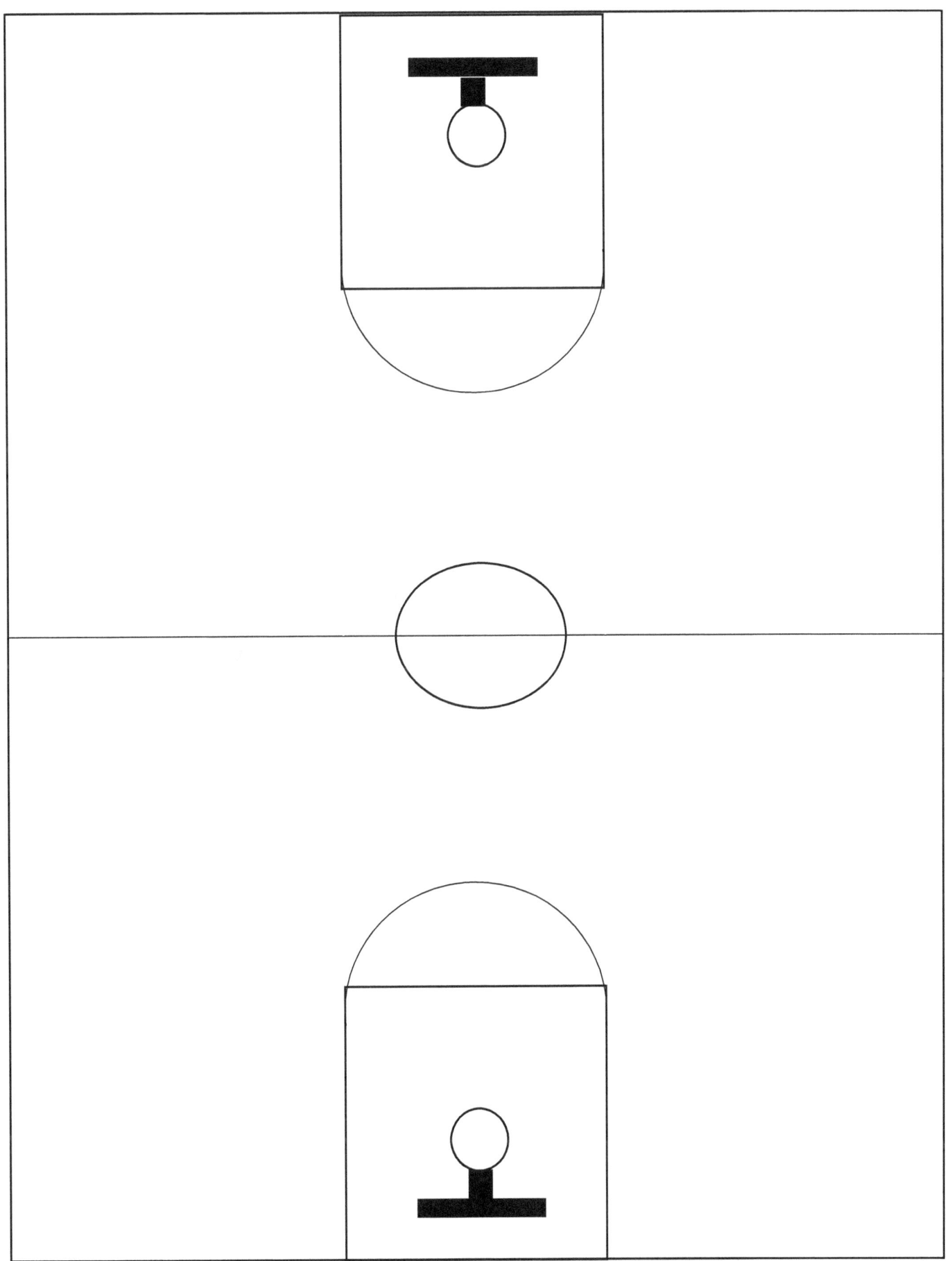

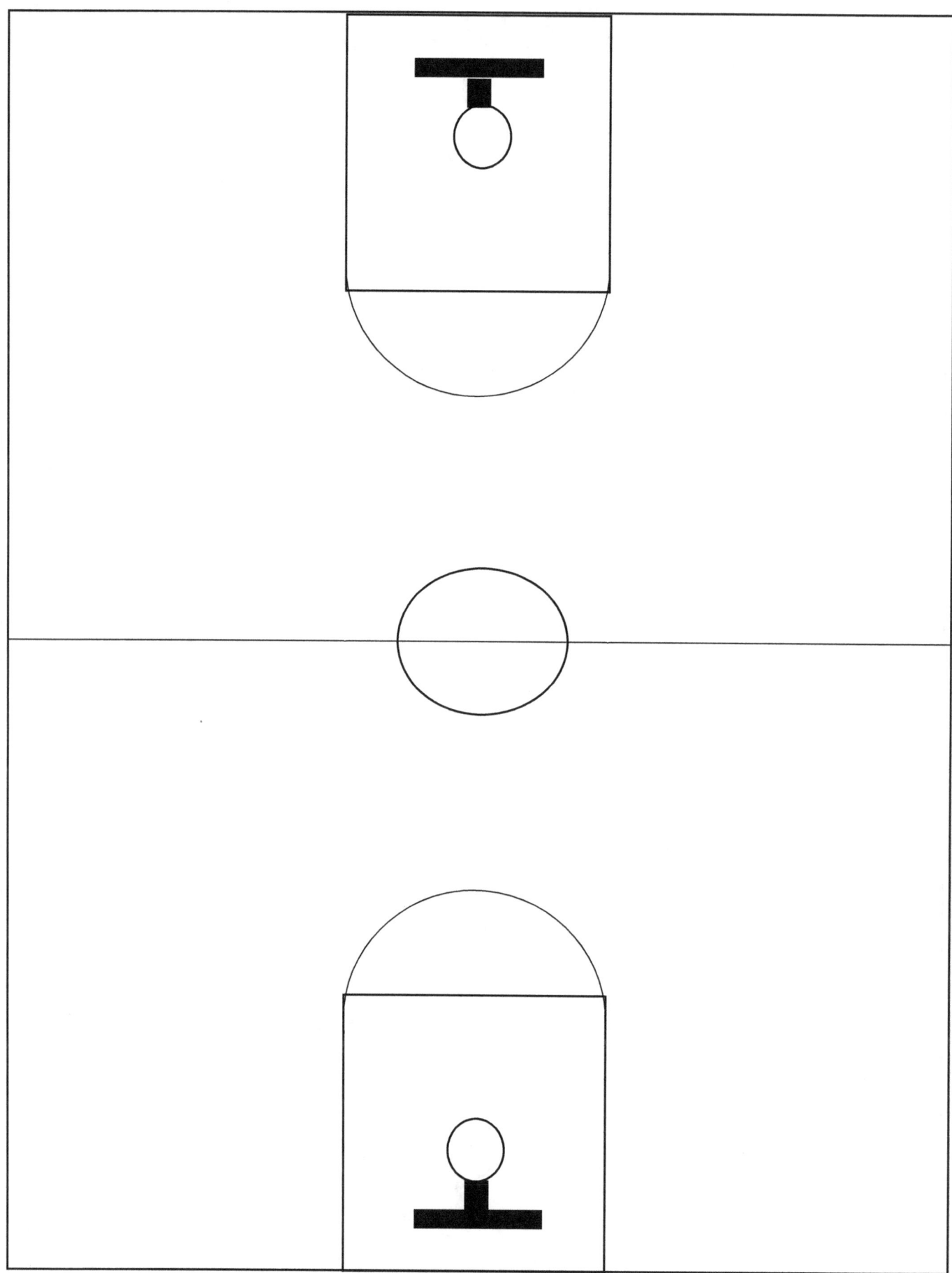

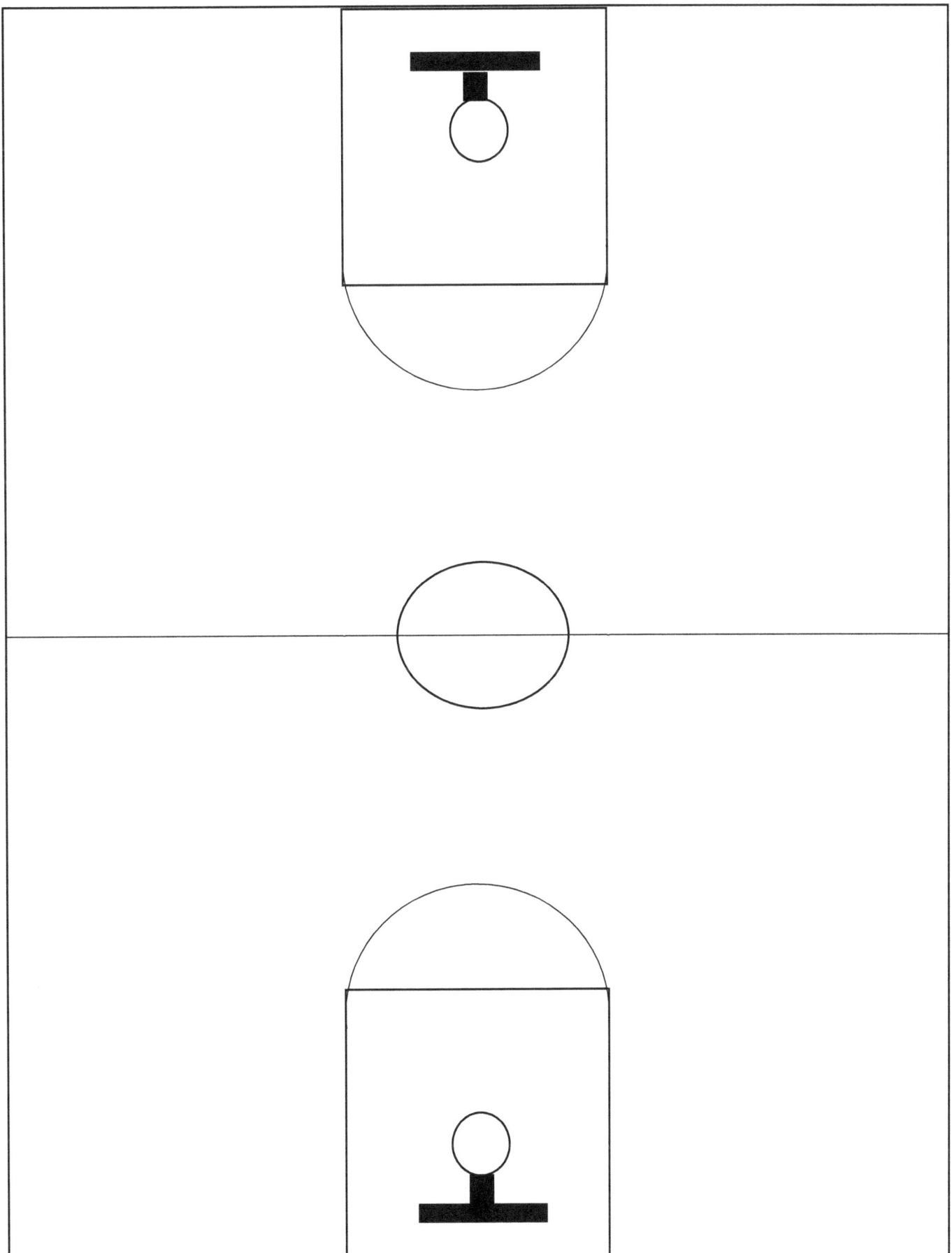

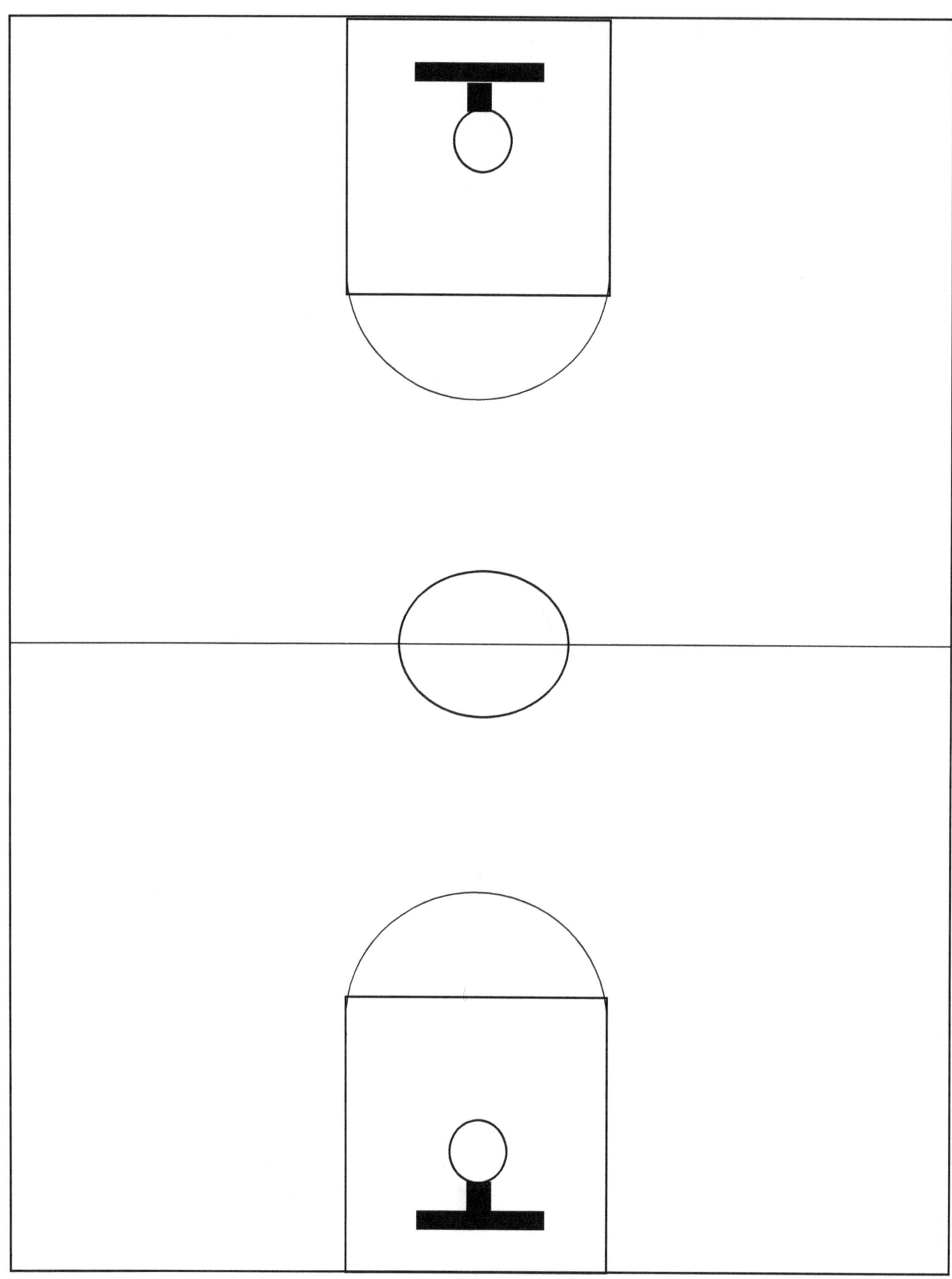

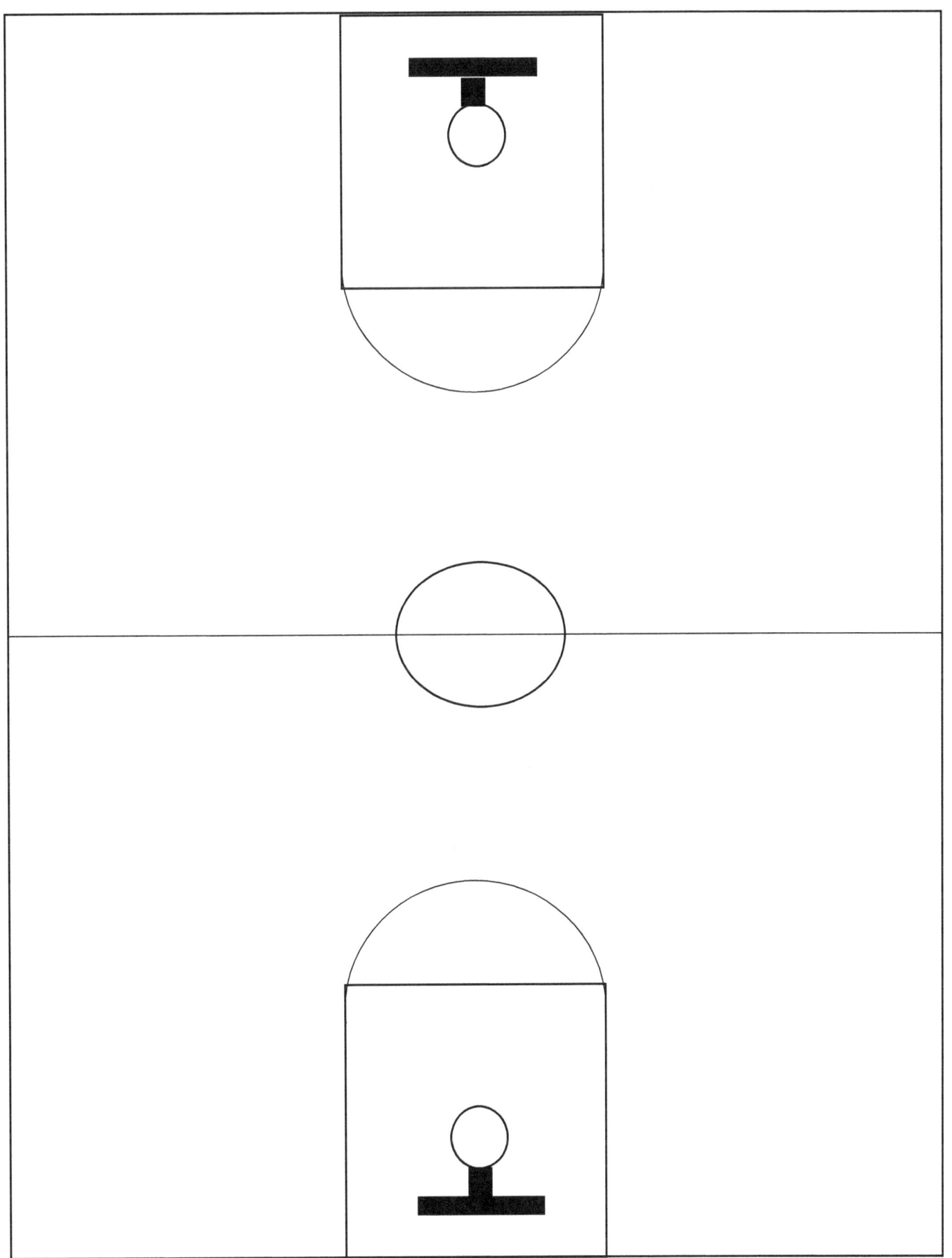

Notes

Notes

Notes

Notes

Notes

Notes

Notes

Notes

Notes

www.ingramcontent.com/pod-product-compliance
Lightning Source LLC
Chambersburg PA
CBHW081232080526
44587CB00022B/3915